How To Draw™ COOL WHEELS

Illustrated by
Jael

kidsbooks Incorporated

Copyright © 2000 Kidsbooks Inc.
3535 West Peterson Ave.
Chicago, IL 60659

Visit us at www.kidsbooks.com
Volume discounts available for group purchases.

INTRODUCTION

This book will show you how to draw lots of different, cool road vehicles. Some are more difficult than others, but if you follow along, step-by-step, you'll soon be able to draw many different things with wheels.

SUPPLIES

NUMBER 2 PENCILS	FELT-TIP PEN
SOFT ERASER	COLORED PENCILS
DRAWING PAD	MARKERS OR CRAYONS

Each vehicle in this book begins with several basic shapes— usually a combination of rectangular and oval shapes. Many variations of these shapes, along with other lines, will also be used.

HELPFUL HINTS

1. In the first two steps of each drawing you will create a solid foundation of the figure (much like a builder who must first construct a foundation before building the rest of the house). Next comes the fun part—creating the smooth, clean outline of the wheeled vehicle, and adding all the finishing touches, such as details, shading, and color.

Note: Following the first two steps carefully will make the final steps easier.

2. **Always keep your pencil lines light and soft.** These "guidelines" will be easier to erase when you no longer need them.

3. **Don't be afraid to erase.** It usually takes a lot of drawing and erasing before you will be satisfied with the way your drawing looks. Each image has special characteristics that make it easier or, in some cases, harder to draw. However, it is easier to draw anything if you first break it down into simple shapes.

4. Add details and all the finishing touches **after** you have blended and refined all the shapes and your drawing is complete.

5. **Remember:** Practice Makes Perfect. Don't be discouraged if you can't get the hang of it right away. Just keep drawing and erasing until you do.

HOW TO START

1. Begin by drawing the basic overlapping shapes, such as the ones in step #1 below, for the general outline of the car. It's usually easier to begin by drawing the largest shape first. The dotted lines show what can be erased as you go along.

2. Sketch the other shapes **over** the first ones. These are the basic guidelines that create the foundation of your drawing.

Remember to keep your lines lightly drawn, and erase any guidelines you no longer need as you go along.

3. Carefully combine and blend all the lines and shapes to create the final outline. Once the car has a smooth, flowing look, begin adding the details that make this cool car unique.

4. Continue to refine your drawing as you darken the tires, add hubcaps, and complete all the finishing touches. When your car is complete, color it with your favorite colors or, for a more dramatic effect, outline it with a thick, black marker.

Use your **imagination** and feel free to create details other than the ones shown. You may even want to add backgrounds to enhance your drawings. When you have drawn some or all of the cool vehicles in this book, and are comfortable with your drawing technique, start creating your own cool wheels!

Most of all, **HAVE FUN!**

1.

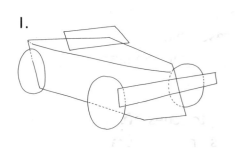

2.

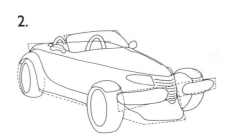

3.

4.

Koenig Porsche 911

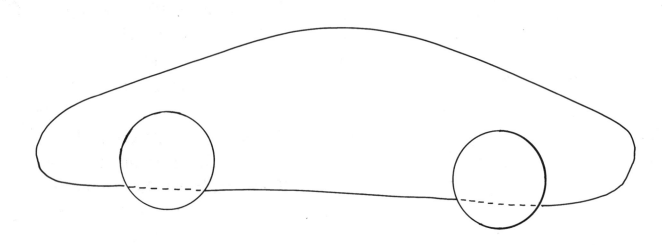

1. Begin by lightly sketching a large, irregular oval guideline shape for the body. Add two circles for the wheels.

   Always keep your pencil lines light and soft, so the guidelines will be easier to erase when you no longer need them.

2. Starting at the front bumper and working up, carefully draw the outline of the upper half of the Porsche. Then do the same for the bottom half. Add the window, tail fin, and inner wheel circles.

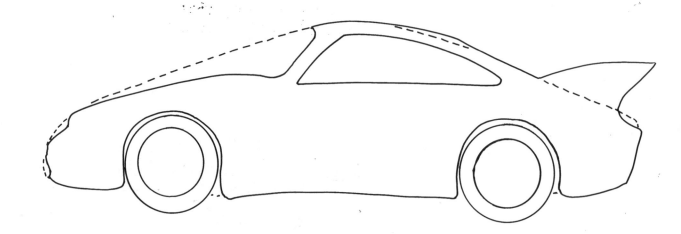

3. Add the windshield, wiper blade, and door. Refine the tail fin and rear-end section. Start adding details.

Remember: Practice Makes Perfect. Don't be discouraged if you can't get the hang of it right away. Just keep drawing and erasing until you do.

4. Draw the headlight, door handles, rear-view mirror, and hubcaps. Darken the tires, and for the finishing touch, outline the car with a thick black line. This will give your Porsche a dramatic look.

DISCARDED

DISCARDED

Cobra

1. Start this hot, little sports car by sketching a large oval shape. Then, add round guidelines for the tires and a rectangular shape for the windshield.

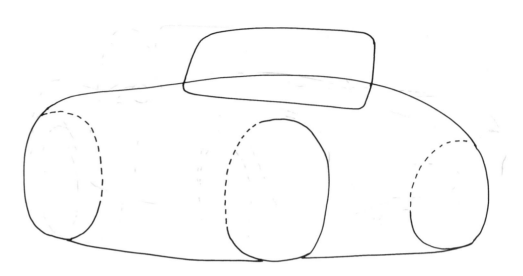

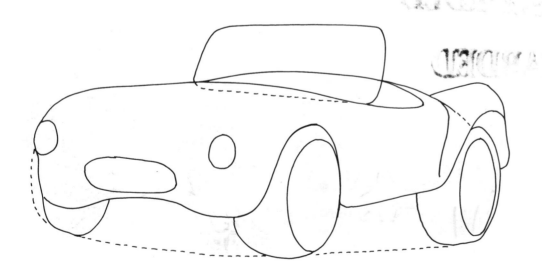

2. Create the tires, including the wheel wells, and shape the basic contour of the Cobra's body, as shown. Add the headlights and grille. Erase any unnecessary lines as you go along.

Note: Take your time doing steps one and two. If you get the basic foundation right, the rest of your drawing will be easy to do.

3. Curve and shape the body into a smooth outline. Note the way the front end dips down. Add guidelines for the door, rear-view mirror, roll bar, air intake, etc.

4. Now comes the fun part—adding all the details that will make this cool car come to life. Create the hubcaps and complete all the body parts. After the details have been refined, darken some of the parts with a black felt-tip pen.

Note: Using a permanent, fine-line marker over your pencil lines will make it easier to erase the guidelines that you no longer need.

Chrysler PT Cruiser

1. Start by lightly sketching the large shape of the body. Add guidelines for the tires and windows.

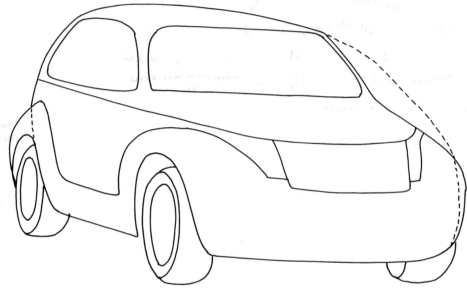

2. Carefully draw the refined outline of the front end. Add the wheel wells and fenders, and start defining and rounding the wheels.

Remember: If you're not satisfied with any part of your drawing, erase it and start over.

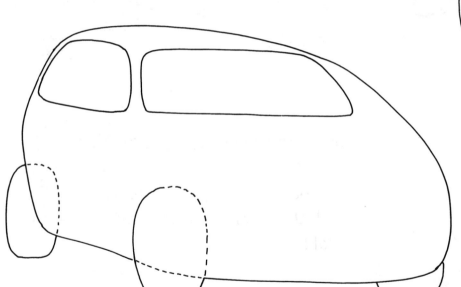

3. Add the doors, lights, bumper, grille areas, and rear-view mirrors. Curve and round all the lines of the car's body shape, erasing any lines you no longer need as you go along. Keep adding and refining all the parts, as shown.

4. Complete the grille, and add the fancy hubcaps and all the other details. Add some dark shading for contrast, and this 2000 sedan-minivan hybrid is ready to roll!

Jaguar XJ 220

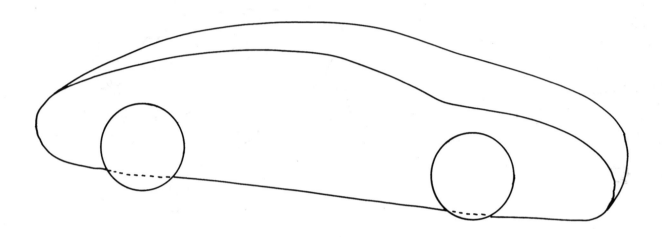

1. Begin with a long horizontal shape for the entire outline of the side of the car. Add the basic circular shapes for the tires. Then, draw another line, from bumper to bumper, above the outline.

Note: This car may seem difficult to draw, but if you follow along step-by-step, you'll soon be able to draw any car you wish.

2. Define the hood, top, and trunk areas. Add the door, inner wheel circles, headlights, and other lines. Now the foundation of your Jaguar is complete.

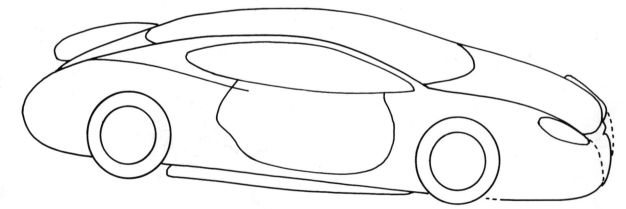

3. Carefully sketch the rear
section, rear-view mirror,
and wheel wells. Refine all
the remaining parts, as
shown. Now you're ready
to add the details and
finishing touches.

4. Create the hubcaps, define
the bumpers, and add the
other details. Outline the
entire car with a thick felt-tip
pen. Then darken the wheels
and interior to complete this
super-cool XJ 220.

Volkswagon Beetle

1. Carefully sketch a large rounded oval for the overall outline of the Beetle. Then add guidelines for the windows, wheels, and bumper.

Remember: Keep all your guidelines lightly drawn. They will be easier to erase later on.

2. Refine the outline into the classic Beetle shape, as shown. Create the hood, fenders, headlights, blinker lights, and rear-view mirrors. Then complete the side panel and tires.

3. Add the hubcaps. Refine and add all the details that will complete your drawing. When you're done, color your Beetle with colored pencils, markers, or crayons.

AM General Hummer

1. Start with a large, lightly drawn rectangular shape for the body. Add the smaller shapes on top and the guideline circles for the wheels.

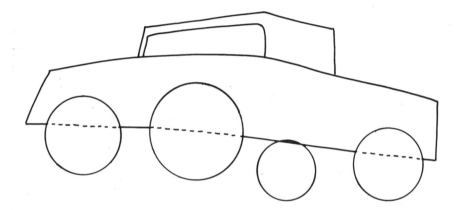

2. Draw the windows and door. Then define the front end by sketching the grille/headlight area. Create the left wheels and wheel wells.

3. Complete the front end. Next, add details such as hubcaps, tire treads, rear-view mirror, windshield wipers, etc. For the final touch, shade-in this cool vehicle with a felt-tip pen.

After your Hummer is complete, add some rough terrain for the Hummer to bounce along on. This heavy-duty, civilian version of the military Humvee can roll over boulders and cross streams two feet deep.

Formula I Race Car

1. Begin this racing car by lightly sketching two large ovals for the huge front tires. Connect them with straight lines. Then add the other overlapping basic shapes and lines.

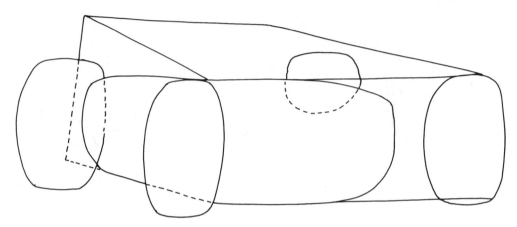

Hint: Did you ever look at something and think it was too difficult to draw? Well, think again. Anything can be drawn if you first examine it carefully and break it down into simple shapes.

2. Add the additional lines that define the overall shape of the car, erasing the guidelines you no longer need.

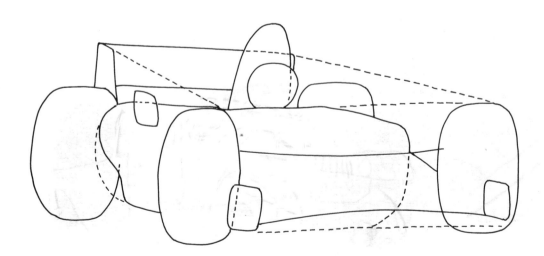

Step #3 is a bit complicated—many parts look like they're just stuck on here and there. So work on one section at a time until you're satisfied with your work.

3. Carefully draw the front end as well as the rods that connect the front tires. Next, draw the section between the front and rear tire. Define the area behind the driver's helmet and the rear end of the racer. Now you're ready to add details.

4. Blacken the tires, and slowly add all the other details, as shown. When your drawing is complete, decorate it with logos and decals of your choice. Next stop: Indy 500!

Dodge Viper

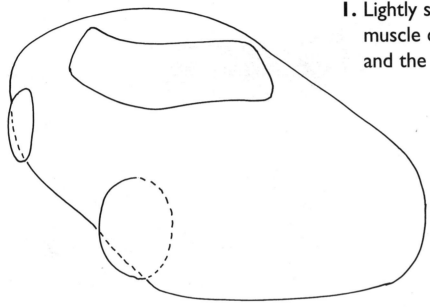

1. Lightly sketch a large irregular oval shape for this muscle car's outline. Add the window sections and the oval shapes for the wheels.

2. Refine the overall body shape. Then draw guidelines for the bumper, headlights, wheel wells, side window, and rear-view mirrors.

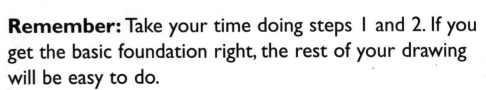

Remember: Take your time doing steps 1 and 2. If you get the basic foundation right, the rest of your drawing will be easy to do.

3. Continue curving all the shapes into a smooth Viper outline. Draw the door and add lines on the top, hood, side, and bumper. Now you can start adding details.

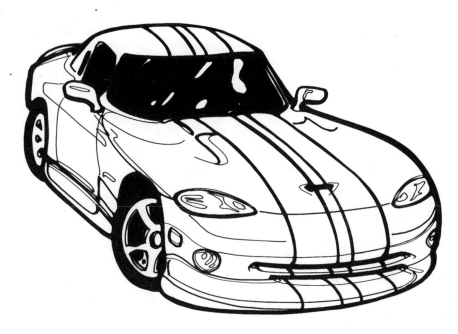

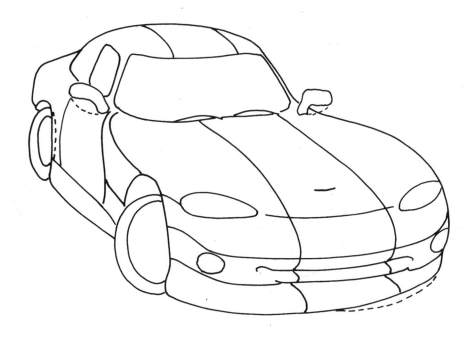

4. Draw the wheel hubcaps. Then darken the interior and add all the finishing touches to complete this cool Viper. A heavy black outline gives this popular sports/race car a dramatic look.

Stock Car Racer

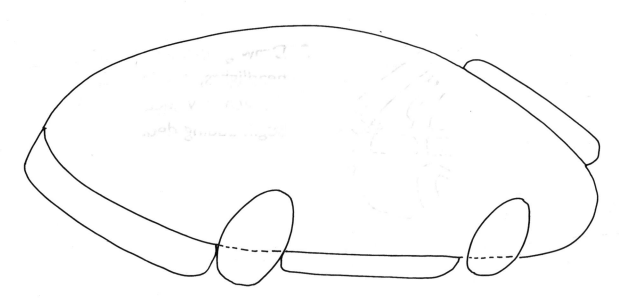

1. These racing machines can go over 200 miles per hour! Start this one by sketching a very large irregular oval shape. Add the additional basic guideline shapes.

Hint: Guideline shapes and lines should always be lightly drawn. They will be easier to erase later.

2. Carefully refine the outline shape of the stock car, creating the front, top, rear and window sections. Now that the foundation of your drawing is complete, make sure you're satisfied with your work before going to the next step.

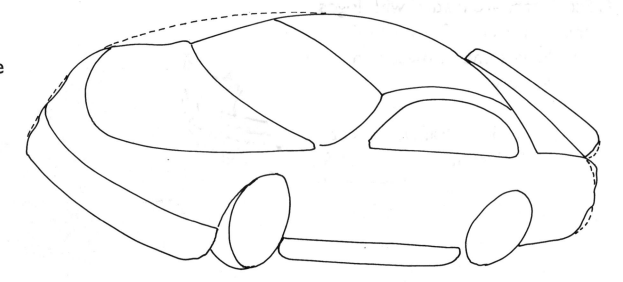

3. Draw guidelines for the grille, headlights, and door. Create the window sections and begin adding details.

4. Stock cars are loaded with logos and decals. Have fun with this one by adding some of these and creating your own.

Hint: For a more dramatic effect, use a thick marker or pen for the outer shape of the stock car and a thin one for the inside lines.

Ford GTO

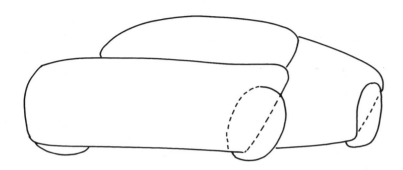

1. Draw the basic shapes for the front end and fenders. Add the guideline shapes for the windshield, side/rear sections, and wheels.

Note: It's easy to draw almost anything if you first build a good foundation.

2. Create the rounded hood and front fenders. Define the side/rear panels, and complete the wheels and wheel wells. Add the vertical rearview mirrors.

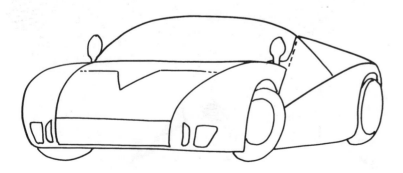

3. Working on one section at a time, draw all the details that make this cool, futuristic GTO one of the hottest cars on the road. Shading and a thick outline give your drawing a dramatic look.

Thrust SSC (Supersonic Car)

1. Clocked at 728 mph, the SSC is the fastest land vehicle ever! Start with a feather-shaped oval for the body. Next, add the two giant overlapping shapes for the huge engines.

2. Draw the inner circles to the engines and the other basic shapes, as shown.

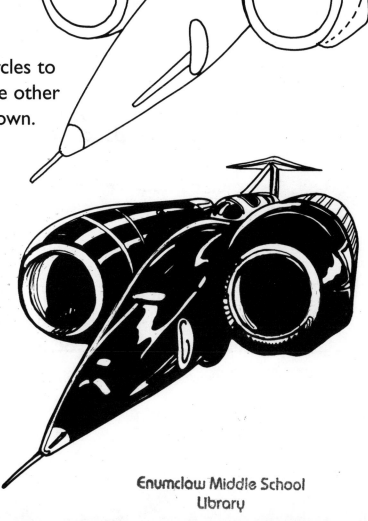

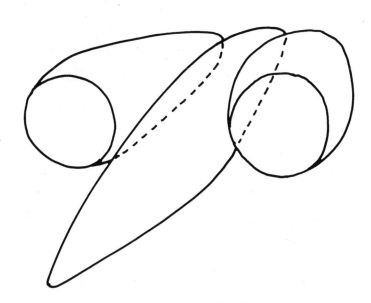

3. Complete the engines and cockpit, and add the part of the wheel that's visible (the wheels are almost scorched off during the runs). Carefully add lots of shading to complete this amazing car.

Plymouth Prowler

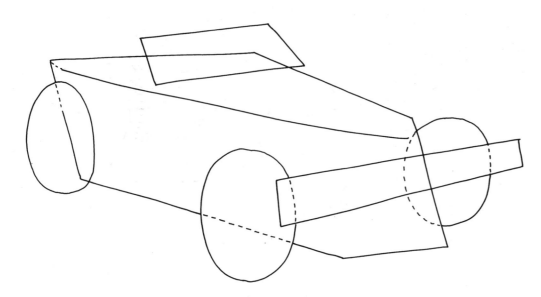

1. Begin by lightly drawing the rectangular and triangular shapes for the body. Add additional guidelines for the windshield, tires, and bumper.

2. Working on one section at a time, round off the overall body shape, including the windshield. Create the fat tires, fenders, grille, and bumpers. Add the remaining parts as shown.

Note: Steps 1 and 2 are very important. They establish the overall structure and look of your drawing. In steps 3 and 4 you are simply refining and adding details to the figure you have created in steps 1 and 2.

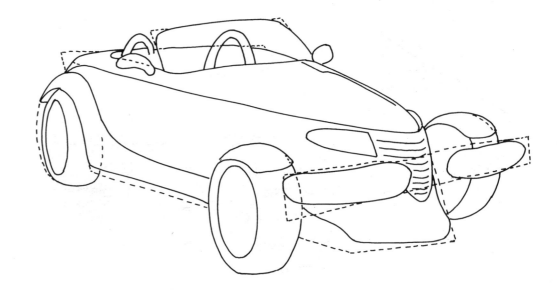

3. Add the door and other details and keep rounding and blending the sections together.

Remember: If you're not satisfied with the way any part of your drawing looks, erase it and start again before going to step #4.

4. Draw the hubcaps, and add all the remaining details that define the Prowler. For the finishing touch, use a heavy felt-tip pen to darken the tires, grille, etc. Then color this factory-made hot rod with your favorite colors.

Ferrari Testarossa

1. Start with a large irregular shape for the front section. Attach the rectangular shape for the side, and connect the two shapes with a long curved line, forming the top. Add guideline shapes for the tires.

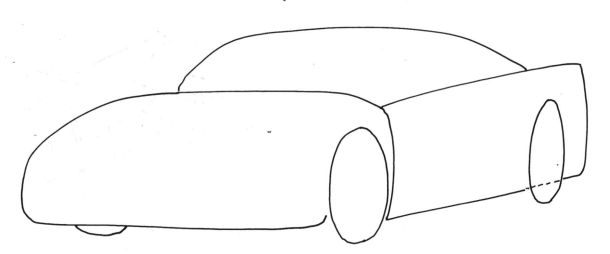

Hint: Look carefully at the drawing and follow along, step-by-step. Even a complicated figure is easier to draw one step at a time.

2. Blend the top into the rear fender, and complete the side panel. Next, create the hood and front end, and draw all the additional lines and shapes, as shown. Carefully sketch the windows, rear-view mirrors, and tires.

3. Continue to refine each part of the body. Note how smooth and rounded all the lines are. Start adding details.

Hint: Wait to add details and all the finishing touches until after you have blended and refined the shapes, and your figure is complete.

4. Complete the door panel, hubcaps, and head lights. When you're finished with details, add shading with a black felt-tip pen. For a dramatic effect, outline the Testarossa with a thick line.

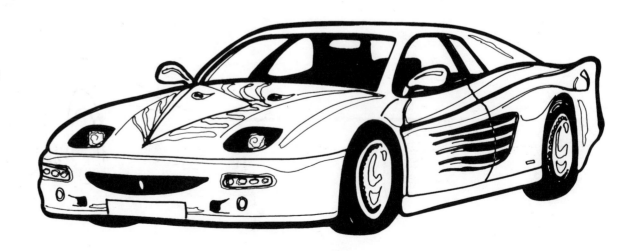

Super SUV

1. Draw the irregular shape for the side of the SUV. Then add the large front section, windshield, top, and wheel guidelines.

Remember: Keep these guidelines lightly drawn. They will be easier to erase later.

2. Work on one section at a time. Round off the front end and create the bumper and grille/headlight section. Then sketch the windshield and small window above it. On the side of the SUV, draw the individual windows, door, wheels and wheel wells, and rear-view mirror.

Note: Make sure you have built a solid foundation with the first two steps before going on to step 3.

3. Continue working on the side section. Note how the windows relate to the roof. Add the door handle, inner wheel lines, and the lines that separate the side panel from the front hood. Complete the hood and front end. Begin adding details.

4. Add the tire treads, hubcaps, and all the finishing touches that make this cool SUV "The King of the Road." When you're satisfied with your drawing, color it with pencils, markers, or crayons.

Corvette Stingray

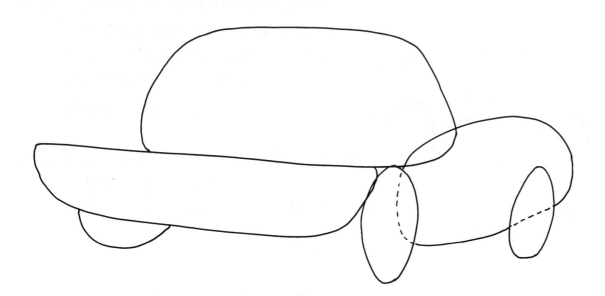

1. Begin by lightly sketching two irregular guideline shapes—one for the top and one for the rear of the Stingray. Add the guideline shapes for the wheels.

Note: It is usually easier to begin with the largest shape first.

2. Draw and connect the rear fenders. Create the side/front fender, the wheels, and the wheel wells. Erase unneeded guidelines as you go along. Add the side and rear windows.

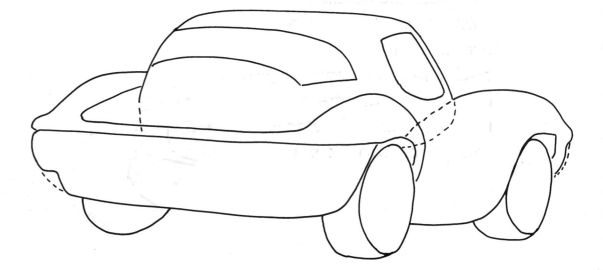

3. Divide the rear window. Then refine and shape all your lines until your drawing has that cool, classic Stingray look. Add the door, two small bumpers, and license plate holder. Then begin adding details.

Remember: Practice makes perfect. Keep drawing and erasing until you are satisfied with the way your Stingray looks.

4. Complete the details. For the finishing touches, darken the tires and windows with a black felt-tip pen. You can also outline the Corvette with a thick black line, or color it with your favorite color.

Vector W8 Twin Turbo

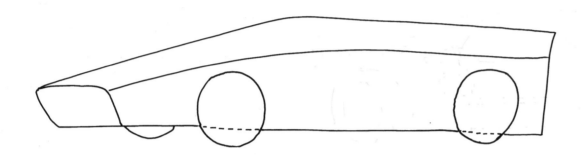

1. It's easier to draw most cars by starting at the front end of the vehicle. Lightly draw the basic guideline shapes of the Vector's long, sleek body sections. Add the tires.

2. Starting at the tip of the front end and ending with the tail fin, create the contours of the hood, top, and rear sections. Erase unneeded guidelines as you go along. Add the windshield, door, and wheel wells.

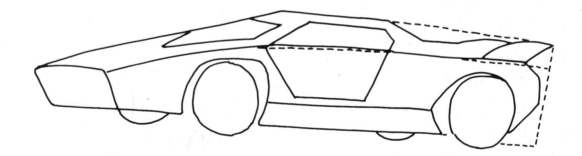

Note: Steps 1 and 2 are very important. They establish the overall structure and look of your drawing. In steps 3 and 4 you are simply refining and adding details to the figure you have created in steps 1 and 2.

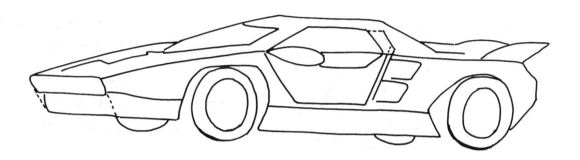

3. Draw the inner wheel circles, the low front-end area, and the rear view mirror. Define each individual section of the Vector by adding all the additional lines and parts, as shown.

4. Sketch the hubcaps, and darken the wheels and wheel wells with a black felt-tip pen. Add details, and for the finishing touch, either outline the Vector with a thick line or color it with your favorite color.

Use this page and your imagination to create the coolest car of your dreams!